The TOWN MOUSE and the COUNTRY MOUSE

Retold by EMMA CARLSON BERNE
Illustrated by JENNIE POH
Music by DEAN JONES

CANTATA LEARNING

WWW.CANTATALEARNING.COM

CANTATA
LEARNING

Published by Cantata Learning
1710 Roe Crest Drive
North Mankato, MN 56003
www.cantatalearning.com

Library of Congress Cataloging-in-Publication Data
Names: Berne, Emma Carlson, author. | Poh, Jennie, illustrator. | Jones, Dean (Musician), music arranger and producer.
Title: The town mouse and the country mouse / retold by Emma Carlson Berne ; illustrated by Jennie Poh ; music by Dean Jones.
Description: North Mankato, Minnesota : Cantata Learning, [2019] | Series: Classic fables in rhythm and rhyme | Summary: A modern song retells the fable of mouse cousins who visit each other's homes, one in the quiet countryside and one in the busy city. Includes a brief introduction to Aesop, sheet music, glossary, discussion questions, and further reading. | Includes bibliographical references.
Identifiers: LCCN 2018026086 (print) | LCCN 2018036286 (ebook) | ISBN 9781684103553 (ebook) | ISBN 9781684103355 (hardcover) | ISBN 9781684103713 (paperback)
Subjects: LCSH: Children's songs, English--United States--Texts. | CYAC: Contentment--Songs and music. | Songs.
Classification: LCC PZ8.3.B45816 (ebook) | LCC PZ8.3.B45816 Tow 2019 (print) | DDC 742.82--dc23
LC record available at https://lccn.loc.gov/2018026086.

Book design and art direction: Tim Palin Creative
Editorial direction: Kellie M. Hultgren
Music direction: Elizabeth Draper
Music arranged and produced by Dean Jones

Printed in the United States of America.
0409

This text is set to the tune of "Oh, My Darling Clementine."

ACCESS THE MUSIC!
SCAN CODE WITH MOBILE APP
CANTATALEARNING.COM

TIPS TO SUPPORT LITERACY AT HOME

WHY READING AND SINGING WITH YOUR CHILD IS SO IMPORTANT

Daily reading with your child leads to increased academic achievement. Music and songs, specifically rhyming songs, are a fun and easy way to build early literacy and language development. Music skills correlate significantly with both phonological awareness and reading development. Singing helps build vocabulary and speech development. And reading and appreciating music together is a wonderful way to strengthen your relationship.

READ AND SING EVERY DAY!

TIPS FOR USING CANTATA LEARNING BOOKS AND SONGS DURING YOUR DAILY STORY TIME

1. As you sing and read, point out the different words on the page that rhyme. Suggest other words that rhyme.
2. Memorize simple rhymes such as Itsy Bitsy Spider and sing them together. This encourages comprehension skills and early literacy skills.
3. Use the questions in the back of each book to guide your singing and storytelling.
4. Read the included sheet music with your child while you listen to the song. How do the music notes correlate to the words of the song?
5. Sing along on the go and at home. Access music by scanning the QR code on each Cantata book. You can also stream or download the music for free to your computer, smartphone, or mobile device.

Devoting time to daily reading shows that you are available for your child. Together, you are building language, literacy, and listening skills.

Have fun reading and singing!

Aesop was a storyteller who wrote hundreds of stories called **fables**. These stories often have animals for characters. Each short story is meant to teach a **moral**, or lesson.

This fable is about two mice with very different lives. A mouse from the quiet countryside visits her cousin, who lives in a fancy house in the busy town. Does the country mouse like the life she finds there? Let's sing together and find out!

With her cousin in the country
a town mouse visited one day.

They ate **acorns** and drank some water.
The town mouse squeaked, "This food is plain."

A quiet life that's full of **safety**
can be as good as fancy things.

Don't run after food and riches
if lots of danger that life brings.

"Come to lunch now at my rich house," the town mouse said. "We eat so fine.

I'll serve you cakes instead of acorns." So they traveled there to **dine**.

A quiet life that's full of safety
can be as good as fancy things.

Don't run after food and riches
if lots of danger that life brings.

At the town house they ate chocolate,
doughnuts, cheese, and buttered bread.

Then two dogs burst through the doorway.
The frightened mice jumped up and **fled**.

A quiet life that's full of safety
can be as good as fancy things.

Don't run after food and riches
if lots of danger that life brings.

The country mouse said, "Goodbye, cousin.
I'm returning to my house.

I've decided I like safety,
and plain food suits a country mouse."

A quiet life that's full of safety
can be as good as fancy things.

Don't run after food and riches
if lots of danger that life brings.

SONG LYRICS

The Town Mouse and the Country Mouse

With her cousin in the country
a town mouse visited one day.
They ate acorns and drank some water.
The town mouse squeaked, "This food is
plain."

A quiet life that's full of safety
can be as good as fancy things.
Don't run after food and riches
if lots of danger that life brings.

"Come to lunch now at my rich house,"
the town mouse said. "We eat so fine.
I'll serve you cakes instead of acorns."
So they traveled there to dine.

A quiet life that's full of safety
can be as good as fancy things.
Don't run after food and riches
if lots of danger that life brings.

At the town house they ate chocolate,
doughnuts, cheese, and buttered bread.
Then two dogs burst through the doorway.
The frightened mice jumped up and fled.

A quiet life that's full of safety
can be as good as fancy things.
Don't run after food and riches
if lots of danger that life brings.

The country mouse said, "Goodbye,
cousin.
I'm returning to my house.
I've decided I like safety,
and plain food suits a country mouse."

A quiet life that's full of safety
can be as good as fancy things.
Don't run after food and riches
if lots of danger that life brings.

The Town Mouse and the Country Mouse

Folk Pop
Dean Jones

Verse

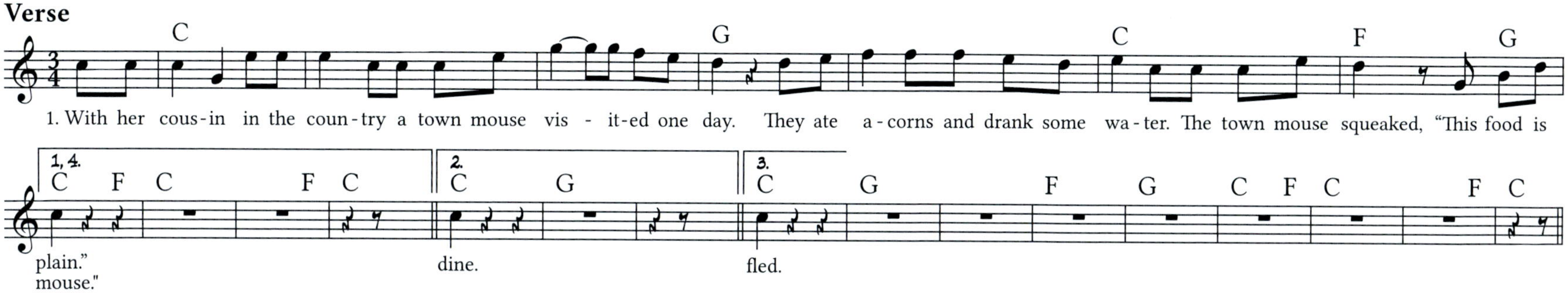

Chorus

Verse 2
"Come to lunch now at my rich house,"
the town mouse said. "We eat so fine.
I'll serve you cakes instead of acorns."
So they traveled there to dine.

Chorus

Verse 3
At the town house they ate chocolate,
doughnuts, cheese, and buttered bread.
Then two dogs burst through the doorway.
The frightened mice jumped up and fled.

Chorus

Verse 4
The country mouse said, "Goodbye, cousin.
I'm returning to my house.
I've decided I like safety,
and plain food suits a country mouse."

Chorus

GLOSSARY

acorns—nuts from an oak tree

Aesop—a legendary storyteller who is said to have lived in ancient Greece around 600 BCE

dine—eat

fables—short stories that often have animal characters and teach a lesson

fled—ran away

moral—a lesson, often found in a fable or story

safety—without danger

CRITICAL THINKING QUESTIONS

1. Why did the town mouse invite the country mouse to visit her in the town? What do you think her goal was?
2. Do you think the country mouse should have gone to the town? Or do you think she should have stayed home?
3. Think of a time when someone invited you to try something new and different. Did you have a good time? Tell what happened.

TO LEARN MORE

Blair, Eric. *The Town Mouse and the Country Mouse*. North Mankato, MN: Capstone Global Library, 2012.

Jacobs, Joseph, ed. *The Fables of Aesop*. Mineola, NY: Dover, 2002.

Rissman, Rebecca. *Mice: Nocturnal Explorers.* North Mankato, MN: Capstone, 2015.

Ward, Helen. *The Town Mouse and the Country Mouse*. Surrey, UK: Templar, 2012.